I Am My Own Best Casual Acquaintance

And Other Cosmic Half-firmations

. . . . .

Shanti Goldstein

CB

CONTEMPORARY
BOOKS

CHICAGO

Caution: This book contains powerful nonprescription
aphorisms. If abused, negative effects on the reader's
chakra, karma, aura, or next reincarnation may result.
The authors offer no warranties of merchantability or
fitness for intended use and advise the reader to seek
the help of a qualified wellness provider in case of
uncontrollable gag reflex.

Published by Contemporary Books, Inc.
Two Prudential Plaza, Chicago, Illinois 60601
Manufactured in the United States of America
Library of Congress Catalog Card Number: 93-17440
International Standard Book Number: 0-8092-3708-3
10   9   8   7   6   5   4   3   2   1

Acknowledgments

*"My life's script is wonderful.
But I have some problems with
the supporting cast."*

We are grateful for the help we've
received from the Universe and Mr. Paul
Hoffman, without whose inspiration this
book would never have levitated off the
ground.

We also must thank our families,
both nuclear and species-wide, for their
invaluable help, even when it was
expressed as an abiding skepticism about
the marketability of this book. As others
have said over and over again, "The
Chinese character for *trouble* is also the

one for *opportunity*." Now we know what they meant.

Thanks, too, to Jorie Rose and Eva Serencsi, whose keen analytical minds revealed every flaw in our work. Also, thanks to Gene Brissie for having the vision to see right through us.

A Message from Shanti

Dear Really, *Really* Close Friend,

You are holding in your hands right now a valuable channel to a new life. You are joining a growing multitude of seekers who are giving birth to themselves, over and over again. As I said once in a previous lifetime, "There's a seeker reborn every minute."

You can avoid all the labor pains with this little but supremely important book! How do you make Half-firmations™ work for you? Each day, turn to a new Half-firmation™. Repeat it to yourself until it's etched indelibly in the appropriate chakra.

Tape it to your computer screen at

work. Make it a part of every memo and fax you send. Inscribe it in bathroom stalls. Write it on your mirror with lipstick. Spray paint it onto the wall of the building next door. Scratch it into the finish of cars that park in your parking space. Everywhere you go, you can spread a soothing, elevating level of consciousness to yourself and the people around you.

Do Half-firmations™ work? Of course they work—*but only if you believe.*

My life, which I want to share with you beyond the boundaries of courtesy and good taste of many other books, is the perfect illustration. Ever since I began inscribing Half-firmations™ into my own line of books, cassettes, videotapes, greeting cards, bumper stickers, message buttons, fortune cookies, outdoor wear, and marital aids, my life has been deeply enriched.

Yours can be, too.

Shanti Goldstein

*You can see
the Universe in
a grain of sand.
Or is it
vice versa?*

If I were not special,
I would not be so near
the top of
the food chain.

*Every day
I love and pleasure myself.
But do I respect myself
in the morning?
And how come I never call?*

Today
I will be open
to whatever the universe
drops on me.

On the fast-paced highway of life, I will strive to be a speed bump.

*Is the glass
half full
or half empty?
And whose lipstick
is on the rim?*

My
personal happiness
depends on
the suffering
of others.

*What gifts am I receiving
from the Universe today?
And what if
they don't fit
or they aren't my color?*

What you hold inside persists.
What you release can clear an elevator.

*Today I will rely
on the language of
love and understanding.
If that doesn't work,
I'll go back to
intimidation and fear.*

*I will strive to
be godlike.
I will start by
condemning
my enemies
to an eternal hell.*

*I listen to my body.
It is saying, "Two
Twinkies and an RC cola,
please."*

*As I learn
to trust the Universe,
I no longer
need to
carry a gun.*

I am
a unique individual,
just like
everybody else.

*All of me
is beautiful
and valuable,
even the
ugly, stupid, and
disgusting parts.*

*I am
at one
with
my duality.*

Blessed are the
flexible,
for they can tie
themselves
into knots.

*I can punish myself
for mistakes of the past—
or I can let
somebody else do it.*

My purpose today
is to share
Peace
with everyone I touch.
And you call that
sexual harassment!

*I cried because
I had no remote control
until I met a man
who had no TV.*

*I will strive to
live each day
as if it were
my fortieth birthday.*

*Life is a
demolition derby,
and I am a Ford Pinto
with Firestone 500 tires.*

"Chop wood, carry water."
But don't expect a tip.

If God did not
want me to
judge and savage myself,
why did S/He
make me so good at it?

*As I let go
of my shoulds
and feelings of guilt,
I can get in touch with
my Inner Sociopath.*

*I have the power
to channel my imagination
into ever-soaring levels
of
suspicion and paranoia.*

*I assume
full responsibility for
my actions,
except the ones
that are
somebody else's fault.*

I no longer need to
punish,
deceive,
or compromise myself.
Unless, of course,
I want
to stay employed.

*In some cultures,
what I do
would be considered
normal.*

*Life
is my school,
and
the vice principal
wants to
see me
in his office.*

*Having control
over myself
is
nearly as good
as having control
over others.*

*If it is natural
to be happy,
why does the
willow weep
and the dove mourn?*

My intuition
nearly makes up for
my lack of
good judgment.

*My Inner Warrior
can kick your
Inner Warrior's ass.*

If God lives within me,
shouldn't I
avoid using antibiotics?

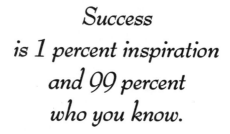

Success
is 1 percent inspiration
and 99 percent
who you know.

*I can change
any thought that hurts
into a reality
that hurts even more.*

*I honor my
personality flaws,
for without them
I would have
no personality at all.*

*I can learn
a lot about myself
by looking into
other people's windows
late at night.*

*Joan of Arc
heard voices, too.*

*The screen
is always darkest
before the
next program
begins.*

I have the choice:
to live my life in wellness
. . . or to get sick
and wallow in all that
attention.

*Hell may be
eternally unpleasant,
but at least
it offers job security.*

Complete honesty
in word and deed
is a good way
to get
punched out.

Without
G-O-D
"good"
would be
"O."

*Today
is the
last day
of your life
so far.*

*No man
is
an isthmus.*

*Today
I will take
my Inner Child
to McDonald's
for a Happy Meal.
Dutch treat.*

When
something
kicks me in the ass,
I will turn the other cheek.

I honor my Inner Warrior. Otherwise he will hurt me. Badly.

There is nothing wrong with me. Really.

Coming out of your shell
is dangerous.
Ask any clam.

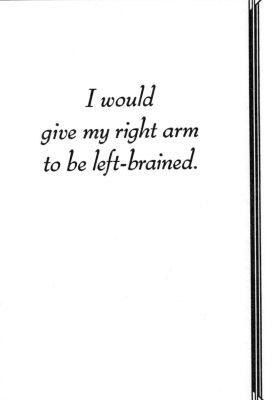

*I would
give my right arm
to be left-brained.*

*Today
I will treat myself
as I would my best friend—
with sarcasm
and neglect.*

*Only
a lack of imagination
saves me
from immobilizing
myself with
imaginary
fears.*

*Today I will
disregard
all negative messages—
like STOP
or YIELD
or WRONG WAY, DO NOT
ENTER.*

*Does my
quiet self-pity
get me to Yes?
Or should I
move up to
incessant nagging?*

*I honor and express
all facets of my being,
regardless of
state and local laws.*

*Life is like the lottery—
the odds are
I'll get back
forty cents for every
dollar I spend.*

*Today
I will gladly
share my
experience and advice,
for there are
no sweeter words
than
"I told you so."*

False hope
is nicer than
no hope at all.

A good scapegoat
is
nearly as welcome
as a
solution to the problem.

Just for today,
I will not sit
in my living room all day,
watching TV.
Instead,
I'll move my TV
into the bedroom.

God is with me
in all circumstances,
at all times,
in all places.
Even Cleveland.

*Am I seeing
and
valuing myself
realistically?
No, thank God!*

*Who can I blame
for my own problems?
Give me just a minute . . .
I'll find someone.*

Why should I
waste time
reliving the past
when I can
spend it
worrying about the future?

*The complete
lack of evidence
is the surest sign
that the conspiracy
is working.*

*I am learning
that criticism
is not nearly as effective
as sabotage.*

*Becoming aware
of my character defects
leads me
to the next step—
blaming my parents.*

*To understand all
is to fear all.*

I will find
humor in
my everyday life
by looking for people
I can laugh at.

The best way
to make my nightmares
come true
is to
wake up.

*I would like to have
the heart
of a small child.
I would keep it
in a jar
on my desk.*

The next time the Universe
knocks on my door
I will pretend
I am not home.

*When I
dance through life,
I do
the Texas Two-Step.*

*My body
is a temple.
Do you want to
come over
for midnight mass?*

The first step is to say nice things about myself.
The second, to do nice things for myself.
The third, to find someone to buy me nice things.

To have a
successful relationship,
I must learn
to make it look
like I'm giving
as much as I'm getting.

*I am willing
to make the mistakes
if
someone else is
willing to learn from them.*

Never judge a man
until you
have driven
a mile on his snow tires.

I am grateful
that I am not as
judgmental
as all those damned
censorious,
self-righteous
people around me.

*If God
wanted us to
trust our own
perceptions,
S/He would not have
given us
organized religion.*

I need not
suffer in silence
while I can still moan,
whimper, and complain.

As I learn
the innermost secrets
of the people around me,
they reward me in many
ways
to keep me quiet.

*If I'm
really quiet
and peaceful
and listen
really hard,
I can hear Howard Stern
in my fillings.*

*When
someone hurts me,
forgiveness
is cheaper
than a lawsuit.
But not nearly as gratifying.*